San Diego's
North County Coast
a photographic portrait

First published in the United States of America by
Twin Lights Publishers, Inc.
10 Hale Street
Rockport, Massachusetts 01966
Telephone: (978) 546-7398
http://www.twinlightspub.com

ISBN 1-885435-26-6

10 9 8 7 6 5 4 3 2 1

Book design by
SYP Design & Production
http://www.sypdesign.com

Cover Photos by: James Blank

Printed in China

Other titles in the Photographic Portrait series:

Cape Ann
Kittery to the Kennebunks
The Mystic Coast, Stonington to New London
The White Mountains
Boston's South Shore
Upper Cape Cod
The Rhode Island Coast
Greater Newburyport
Portsmouth and Coastal New Hampshire
Naples, Florida
Sarasota, Florida
The British Virgin Islands
Portland, Maine
Mid and Lower Cape Cod
The Berkshires
Boston
Camden, Maine

contents

acknowledgment

Twin Lights Publishers would like to thank all of the photographers who submitted their work for our consideration. Because of space limitations, we were unable to include many excellent photographs in *San Diego's North County Coast: A Photographic Portrait.* The North County Coast of San Diego is a wonderful area for many talented professional and amateur photographers. The natural beauty and abundant activities attract visitors and residents to record its special qualities throughout the year.

Special thanks to Ann L. Hurd who organized and supervised the photography contest. A special word of thanks to the camera stores who made the fliers available to their customers and to Sandy Helt for introducing Ann to the vast arena of San Diego Camera Clubs.

Thanks for the expert help of George and Gale Hurd who assisted with the preliminary sorting and judging of over 500 photographs.

Thank you to the judges of the San Diego's North County Coast Regional Photograph Contest, Pamela Boyle, Lin Craft, Melissa Langham, and Jay Langham. We are pleased with their selections and are indebted to them for their efficiency and expertise.

We extend our appreciation to James Blank of Scenics of America, P. O. Box J, Chula Vista, California, 91912 for providing aerial photographs representing the variety of areas along the North County Coast.

We are grateful to Jeanne Reed and Ann Hurd for collaborating on the caption writing. Even though a picture is worth a thousand words, we feel the captions and titles have added a plethora of unique facts and colorful dimensions to the book.

Finally, our thanks go to designer Sara Day whose talent and wonderful sense of continuity and vision have created another beautiful book.

This artistic full color photographic record covers San Diego's North County Coast and includes the beaches and communities of La Jolla, Torrey Pines, Del Mar, Cardiff-by-the-Sea, Encinitas, Solana Beach, Leucadia, Carlsbad and Oceanside. These 150 color images have been selected from over 500 photographic entries. They portray the diverse settings, activities, seascapes and landscapes that have made the North County Coast so enticing to residents and visitors alike.

More than any other photo book published on this region, *San Diego's North County Coast: A Photographic Portrait* shows why these beaches and communities are so special. From aerials of each community, to your favorite beach, to close-ups of beautiful flowers, to magnificent sunsets, this book shows you why tourists come to visit and why residents are happy to call this area home.

Lin Craft

Melissa Langham

Jay Langham

judges

Lin Craft
Lin is an avid photographer who is president of the Southern California Association of Camera Clubs (SCACC). Lin has earned many awards in the area of photography. She is a Fellow of SCACC and an Associate of the Photographic Society of America. She has judged many local, national and international competitions and salons. Lin is a marine biologist and as such has developed a love of underwater photography. She has made over 4500 underwater dives, some of which have been at the North Pole. Lin has graciously allowed us to use this beautiful photograph of ranunculus blossoms as a sample of her work.

Pamela Boyle
Pamela is a long time aficionado of the arts and photography. She has lived in the San Diego area for over twenty-five years. During that time she has made a point to get to know every square inch of the beaches and communities surrounding her home. She is truly an expert on the diverse aspects of the coastal towns of the North County Coast.

Melissa Langham
Melissa has a B.A. degree in Journalism with an emphasis in photojournalism from San Diego State University. Since then, she has always made her livelihood as a professional photographer. Over the years, photography to Melissa is a way of striving for the connecting thread of form and content in all that she presents. Melissa has allowed us to publish one of her beautiful Polaroid manipulation photographs done on Time-Zero film.

Jay Langham
Jay received his A.A. degree from Grossmont College where an appreciation of photographic art began. He has his own home-based photographic studio in Rancho San Diego. Most of his work has been with traditional black and white processes and within the last three years he began working with the unique versatility of digital imaging. Jay has lent us one of his digital renditions of a beautiful coastal scene. Melissa and Jay can be reached at www.langhamphoto.com.

first place

Lindsey Padgett

CANON REBEL G
FUJI VELVIA
F 5.6

Soaring High

Adventurous paragliders soar above the 360-foot Torrey Pine cliffs. The judges felt that this photographer captured all the elements of a great photograph, while depicting the adventure and beauty that is found along the San Diego North County Coast.

Since a very young age, Lindsey Padgett has held a great appreciation for art, photography and nature. Her true love for photography began in 1997 when she and her husband embarked upon a cross-country road trip from Ohio to San Diego, where they were relocating. The road trip experience brought out her desire to capture all of the beauty that engulfs America in order to share it with others. Not long after, she purchased a good SLR camera and taught herself how to use it through books and the use of the internet. Now, she photographs with her husband as they take many scenic photo excursions around San Diego, the state of California and the West. They joined a photo club in 2000 and have since expanded their photography to include flower and macro photography. Her goals for the coming year are to photograph more animals and people. Lindsey is constantly motivated and inspired to improve and to try new things in the area of photography.

second place

Lindsey P. Martin
CANON A 2/28-105MM
FUJI VELVIA
F 22

Broken Hill Sunrise

A favorite spot of photographers near and far, this prize-winning photo is enhanced by the intensity of the morning sun shining on the ridges of Broken Hill.

With a love of nature and travel, Lindsey P. Martin uses photography as a tool to express her creativity and to celebrate the beauty of the natural world. She enjoys capturing special moments and special places on film, and sharing them with others. Her images have been published on greeting cards, in calendars, books, and magazines, including *Nature's Best, Nature Photographer, National Wildlife* and *National Geographic Traveler.* A native of Southern California, Lindsey currently resides in the colorful canyon country of Southwestern Utah, where she teaches photography workshops. Lindsey can be contacted at lindsey-martin@earthlink.net.

Jim Cline
CANON EOS-3
KODAK E100VS
F 5.6 1/30 SEC.

Sunset at Oceanside Pier

Clouds take free rein across the
sky as the sun sets behind
Oceanside Pier. Surfers paddle in
from catching the last waves
before nightfall.

Jim is an award-winning travel
photographer based in San
Diego, California. His wanderlust
and search for compelling images
has taken him to 30 countries
and 6 continents around the
globe. He especially enjoys
exploring less traveled areas,
photographing the indigenous
peoples and traditional cultures
found in developing nations.
Although he usually photographs
while traveling, at times he
points his lens at some of San
Diego's natural wonders.
"Sometimes when you live in a
place it's easy to take it for
granted, even one as diverse
with as many photographic possi-
bilities as San Diego County,"
said Jim. "But when I take my
camera out for a day here, I am
seldom disappointed."

la jolla

Sea Wall

Ryan Kelly

NIKON F100
SENSIA II 100
F5.6, 1/1000

Waves roar across the seawall at Children's Pool.

Lookout

Bill Remlinger

NIKON N90S/35-70MM
FUJI SENSIA
F8 1/250

Breathtaking ocean vistas along the curved walkway
stop visitors and locals alike as they gaze in awe at
nature's wonders.

Basking in the Setting Sun

Marie Tartar

NIKON N90S
SENSIA
F8

California sea lions, protected at La Jolla's Children's Pool, loll in the light of the setting sun.

Lacy Eucalyptus

Marie Tartar

NIKON N90S
SENSIA
F8

Eucalyptus trees are silhouetted by a summer sky above the waters off La Jolla Shores Drive.

(opposite)
La Jolla Cove

Ryan Kelly

NIKON F100
SENSIA II 100
F8, 1/4

A lone seagull soars above, while the pinks and lavenders of the setting sun reflect serenely on the wet sand and the cliffs of La Jolla Cove.

Moonlight Surf

Steve Abuzzo
NIKON N-90 80-200MM

A lone surfer ponders the force of the waves before he
enters the evening surf.

Picture Frame

Steve Abuzzo

NIKON N-90 28-105MM

Mussel encrusted pilings along Scripps Pier
frame the pounding sea.

(opposite)

Jeweled Cliffs
Honorable Mention

James Blank

PENTAX 67
FUJI VELVIA
F11 1/60

This serene setting of the La Jolla coastline is highlighted by yellow gazanias as seen from the cliffs looking north from the coast walk.

Coast Walk

James Blank

PENTAX 67
EKTACHROME 64
F22 1/30

Varying ocean depths cause waves to break unevenly as they roll towards the shoreline at the La Jolla Beach and Tennis Club. When waves are high, surfers enjoy the thrill of riding the length of the waves all the way to the rocky coast.

(previous page)
Siesta Time

Bill Remlinger

NIKON N90S/35-70MM
FUJI SENSIA
F8 1/250

Oblivious to the crashing waves on the break wall, these sea lions bask in the sun at Children's Pool.

Nestled on Rock

Bill Remlinger

NIKON N90S/500 MM
FUJI VELVIA
F8 1/500

A Brown Pelican basks on his throne.

Perfect Landing
Honorable Mention

Bill Remlinger

NIKON N90S/300 MM
FUJI VELVIA
F4 1/1000

A Brown Pelican floats gracefully to his landing pad on the rocks above La Jolla Cove.

(opposite)
Stately

Bill Remlinger

NIKON N90S/500MM
FUJI VELVIA
F5.6 1/500

In mating plumage, this Brown Pelican is perched on a cliff at La Jolla Cove.

Winged Garibaldi
Honorable Mention

Diane Hotz

NIKON 50/SEA N SEA HOUSING
PROVIA 100
F8/SB105STROBE

A garibaldi drifts effortlessly through the deep blue sea. The garibaldi is protected off the California coast because it is extremely territorial and can be easily hunted.

Garibaldi

Shirley A. Reynolds

CANON EOS A2E
KODAK E100VS

A brilliant orange garibaldi appears frozen in time as he guards his domain from the eyes of human intruders.

(opposite)

Cove in Winter

James Blank

LINHOF TECHNIKA
EKTACHROME 64
F22 1/60

A rich tapestry of red torch lilies enhances the view as visitors stand atop La Jolla Cove to watch the pounding surf continuing its relentless destruction and remolding of the coastline.

Lost But Not Forgotten

James Blank

PENTAX 67
EKTACHROME X
F11 1/125

This natural arch at La Jolla Cove was a landmark until it collapsed in a storm in the 1970's. Visitors from far and wide who long ago marveled at the scene recall with fond memories the beauty that once was.

(opposite)
Natural Arch Frame

James Blank

LINHOF TECHNIKA
EKTACHROME 64
F32 1/30

Low lying clouds at Torrey Pines are framed by the rugged formation of a natural arch carved over millions of years by the unrelenting sea.

Dancing Prints

Tiger Lee
OLYMPUS E10 DIGITAL

A mother and two daughters stroll along the shore as twilight approaches.

(left)

Mount Soledad

Mary L. Thompson
CANON REBEL G

This 43-foot high cross stands above San Diego and La Jolla on Mount Soledad and can be seen from miles around. Visitors to the area enjoy a 360-degree panoramic view of the San Diego area. The cross was built in 1954 in honor of the many men and women who died in the service of their country.

(below)

Surreal World

Ryan Kelly
NIKON F100
SENSIA II 100
F16

Lights along the shore appear as diamonds in the night reflecting the upscale La Jolla lifestyle. A timed exposure evokes an ethereal appearance on the water and in the sky above. La Jolla means the jewel in Spanish and was named for its radiant beauty.

"Spring Stirring"

Gunnar Ostrand

NIKON N70/28-200MM
FUJI SENSIA
F8

Sculpture by San Diego artist Donal Hord entitled
"Spring Stirring" overlooks the Pacific from the
University of California at San Diego's Scripps Institute
of Oceanography.

(opposite)
Nitetime Splendor

Thomas J. Kovtan

NIKON N90S
FUJI REALA
F16

Just to the east of Interstate 5 at Nobel Drive stands
one of the crown jewels of the La Jolla skyline, the
Mormon Temple. The twin 190-foot towers with their
multifaceted windows highlight the evening sky and
dazzle travelers.

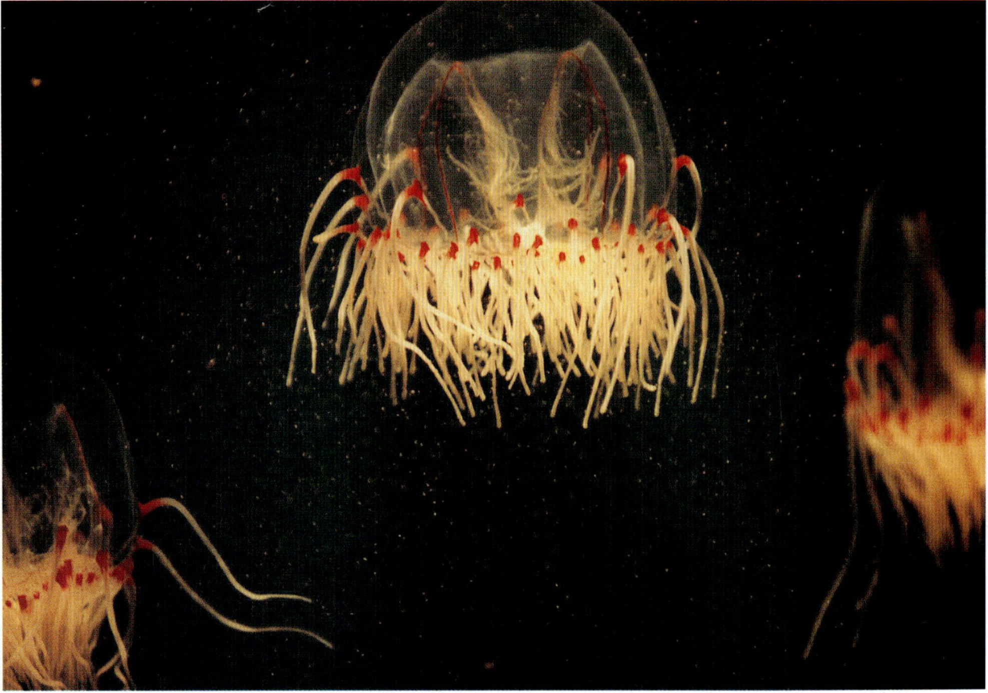

Lion Fish

Carol Cirone

CANON 1-N 50MM
PROVIA 100

A lionfish lounges on the soft coral at the Stephen Birch Aquarium at Scripps Institution of Oceanography. Lionfish are given wide berths as divers explore the colorful waters around the aquarium.

(left)
Dancing Jellyfish

Caroline E. Brown

NIKON F100
VELVIA

Visitors watch as gold and red Jellyfish perform effortlessly with their tentacles glowing in the dark of the underwater the-atre at Stephen Birch Aquarium. The aquarium is part of Scripps Institution of Oceanography which was founded in 1903. The aquarium moved into updated facilities in 1992.

La Jolla Denizen

Carol Cirone

CANON ELAN 75-300MM
PROVIA 100

Just below Ellen Browning Scripps Park a sea lion
cub slumbers.

(top)

White Wall

Carol Cirone

CANON 1-N 75-300MM
PROVIA 100

Turbulent waves made it difficult
for this surfer to advance into
the waters at Windansea Beach.

(bottom)

Knee Boarding

Carol Cirone

CANON 1-N 75-300MM
VELVA PUSHED 1

Knee boarding at Windansea
Beach in La Jolla is a popular style
of surfing in the California sun.

Jeweled Sea

Isabella Breasted

NIKON 6006 300MM
KODAK 200
AUTO

Visitors frolic along the narrow beach as waves roll gently to the rocky shore. The changing depths of the ocean floor can be seen through the varying hues of the sea.

Glistening Image

Caroline E. Brown

NIKON F100
VELVIA

The waters off Black's Beach provide a glistening backdrop for a lone swimmer.

Winged Flight

Caroline E. Brown

NIKON F100
VELVIA

Pelicans take flight among the wispy clouds above the waters of La Jolla Cove. Sunset is an excellent time to catch a view of the majestic birds as they search for that last meal of the day.

Spotlight on the Pier

Isabella Breasted

NIKON 6006 300MM
KODAK 200
AUTO

Waves during a winter storm greet visitors to the
La Jolla Caves.

torrey pines

Moonlike Crater

Rick Wiley

Sunrise is the best time to capture the rich amber
tones of the sandstone that mimics a crater on
the moon.

(opposite)

Golden Sandstone

Geoff Shester

CANON A-1
FUJI PROVIA 100
F5.6

At Torrey Pines State Reserve, cliffs of golden sandstone embrace the warmth of the sunlight.

Black's Beach

Garry Belinsky

NIKKORMAT 100MM
E100VS
2.8

An evening sun warms the sandstone cliffs as waves
slip onto the shore at Black's Beach.

(opposite)
Sunset Runner

Zackery Birdsell

NIKKORMAT 100MM
E100VS
2.8

A solitary runner goes for run on Black's Beach in
Torrey Pines.

Hup, Two, Three

Goran Matijasevic
CANON EOS A2
EKTACHROME 100

Sandpipers march in formation to investigate the puddles left by the tide.

(opposite)
Lone Surfer

Richard Grafton
NIKON F-5
PROVIA 100F
F22

A surfer basks in the glow of the evening sunset.

Eroded Cliffs

James Blank

MAMIYA C330
EKTACHROME 64
F16 1/60

The contrasting hues of the calm blue waters appear to defy the barren cliffs as the land reaches out to meet the sea.

(previous page)

Cliff Trails

Geoff Shester

CANON A-1
FUJI VELVIA
F11

A favorite weekend outing for families is a walk along the beach and up the trails leading to the cliff overlooks above Torrey Pines State Reserve.

Sculpted Bluff

James Blank

PENTAX 67
EKTACHROME 64
F16 1/60

The sculpted bluffs of sandstone appear as a formidable sentry standing guard against the pounding surf on a beach at Torrey Pines State Park.

Torrey Pines Golf Course

James Blank

LINHOF TECHNIKA
EKTACHROME 64
F22 1/30

The lush green slopes of the renowned Torrey Pines Municipal Golf Course host the PGA Tour's Buick Invitational as well as providing an affordable recreational playground for local golfers.

(opposite)
Golfer's Dream

James Blank

LINHOF TECHNIKA
EKTACHROME 64
F22 1/30

Each year when the PGA is broadcast across the world, golfers dream of playing the picturesque course and sinking a ball on the pristine greens at Torrey Pines Golf Course.

Sunrise at Broken Hill

Bill Remlinger
NIKON FE2/35-70 MM
FUJI VELVIA
F11 1/30

These torrey pines are perched on the sandstone of
Broken Hill in the Torrey Pines Reserve. Found only in
two locations in the world, there are over 4000 of the
trees here, with the oldest being 130 years old.

(opposite)
Inviting Trail

James Blank
PENTAX 67
EKTACHROME 64
F22 1/30

A favorite hiking trail in Torrey Pines Reserve leads
to the ocean below through a winding and rugged
terrain dotted with torrey pines.

Romance in the Air

Lindsey P. Martin

CANON A2/17-35MM
FUJI ASTIA
F22

High tides have left puddles which reflect the sunset among the scattered beach rocks.

(left)

Moonrise

Jim Cline

CANON EOS-3
KODAK E100VS
F8 AT 8 SEC.

The moon rises above a bold sunset at Penasquitos Lagoon.

Sunset at Penasquitos Lagoon

Jim Cline
CANON EOS-3
KODAK E100VS
F5.6 1/15

A family stands framed by the symmetrical pattern of
the Pacific Coast Highway Bridge.

Torrey Pines Glider Port

Garry Belinsky
NIKKORMAT 100MM
E100SW
2.8

A bystander looks on as a paraglider prepares for a lift
off from the cliffs above Black's Beach.

Up, Up, and Away

Richard E. Leffler

CANON A1 300 MM
SENSIA 100
F8

At Torrey Pines Glider Port, the action of the gentle
winds against the bluffs provides ideal conditions
for soaring.

Sunset Silhouettes

Geoff Shester

CANON A-1
FUJI VELVIA
F16

Twin yuccas stand at attention while awaiting nightfall.

(left)
Majestic Fire

Lindsey P. Martin

CANON A2/28-105MM
FUJI
F16

The red glow of the sunset reflects its majestic fire on the pebbles along the beach.

Firey Sunset

Carol Cirone

CANON I-N 75-300MM
PROVIA 100

Drifting smoke from an East San Diego County fire
makes for a dramatic sunset

Sunset on Coast Highway

Isabella Breasted

NIKON 6006 300 MM
KODAK 200
AUTO

The evening sun highlights the contours of the bridge on old highway 101 as you travel south towards Torrey Pines State Reserve. The tall buildings of La Jolla's skyline can be seen in the distance.

Old Highway 101

Isabella Breasted

NIKON 6006 300 MM
KODAK 200
AUTO

The narrow strand of sand in the background, north of Torrey Pines State Beach, is a favorite for beachgoers and surfers. The waters from Penasquitos Lagoon run into the ocean from under the bridge on old Highway 101.

(opposite)

Ageless Beauty

James Blank

LINHOF TECHNIKA
EKTACHROME 64
F22 1/30

Over the centuries erosion has scarred the bluffs of the Torrey Pines Reserve.

Posing

Caroline E. Brown

NIKON F - 100
VELVIA

A young seagull chick poses for
the camera, his bright orange
beak contrasting with his downy
gray feathers.

(right)
Gridlock

Paul Shilling

CANON REBEL X
FUJI SUPER G

A flock of seagulls bask in the
evening sunlight undisturbed by
visitors to the beach.

(opposite)
Torrey Pine's Eye View

Michael Boidy

SEURS SLR
FJUI 100
F16

Branches of a torrey pine frame
one of the numerous hiking trails.

(top)

Frolicking

Caroline E. Brown

NIKON F - 100
VELVIA

Youngsters play a game of
"catch me if you can" with
seagulls along the rocky beach
at Torrey Pines.

(bottom)

Thundering Serenity

Roger Alther

MINOLTA X700
FUJI 200
F8

A thundering locomotive breaks
the early morning calm as a grand-
mother and her grandson explore
the marshes of Penasquitos Lagoon.

Mirror Image

Caroline E. Brown

NIKON F - 100
VELVIA

A young whimbrel searches for a tasty tidbit in the wet
sand while his mirrored twin looks on with interest.

del mar

solana beach

cardiff-by-the-sea

Perpetual Motion
Honorable Mention

Carol Cirone

CANON ELAN
VELVIA PUSH 1X

A merry go round of lights collide as two midway rides spin and loop in this timed exposure shot at the Del Mar Fair.

(left)
Fun Zone

Shirley A. Reynolds

CANON EOS A2E LONG EXPOSURE
KODAK E100VS
TRIPOD

Thousands of visitors flock to the Del Mar Fair every summer. At night the fun zone at the fair comes alive with people and lights.

(opposite)
Sunset Lava Flow
Honorable Mention

Lindsey P. Martin

CANON A2/28-135MM
KODAK E100VS
F16

A combination of bronzed wet sand and sunken rocks emulate molten lava flowing over the landscape.

4th of July

Thomas J. Kovtan

NIKON N6006
FUJI 100
F8

From the middle of June until the 4th of July,
people of all ages enjoy the Del Mar Fair. This
traditional fair is one of the largest in the
country and provides fun for all, as depicted
in this photo of an oversized clown dazzling
onlookers.

Human Ballast

Thomas J. Kovtan

NIKON N6006
FUJI 100
F5.6

Balloonists hold on tightly as a colorful hot air
balloon is being prepared for take off. On
many late afternoons, dozens of balloons are
launched from various vacant lots in the Del
Mar Area.

Ready for Take Off

Gunnar Ostrand

NIKON N70/28-200MM LENS
FUJI SENSIA
F11

Colorful hot air balloons prepare to take off
south of Rancho Santa Fe. The onshore winds
and the magnificent views are two of the fac-
tors that make the Del Mar and Rancho Santa
Fe areas ideal for hot air ballooning.

Coastal Colors

Geoff Shester

CANON A1
FUJI PROVIA
F16

People gather at the Del Mar beaches to
watch as the sun goes down. Purple Statice is
found along most of the beach walks in the
San Diego area.

(top)

Shoreline Supper

Richard E. Leffler

CANON A1 300 MM
SENSIA 100
F8

Common sights along the
coastal beaches near Del Mar
are seagulls searching for hand-
outs by visitors.

(bottom)

Around the Turn

Richard E. Leffler

CANON A1/100- 300 DOUBLER
SENSIA 100

It is quite a challenge to secure
a spot at the Del Mar Race Track
to photograph horses coming
directly towards the camera.
The photographer found the
perfect spot for this action
packed photo.

Playful Dogs

Lindsey P. Martin

CANON A2
KODAK E100VS
F8

This pair of playful dogs are enjoying the late
afternoon at Del Mar's Dog Beach. Dogs are allowed
off their leashes during certain hours and times of
the year.

Pooches Playground

Joanne Max

CANON EOS 3
FUJICOLOR NPS
F11

Dog Beach is a canine playground where a dog can be a dog. Dogs are not allowed on most beaches in the San Diego area, however, dogs can play freely along this beach and visit with other doggy friends. Leashes are sometimes required as evidenced in these photos.

Backlit Blossom

Marie Tartar

NIKON N90S
SENSIA
F32

The Jimson Weed, with its beautiful white blossoms, grows in the San Elijo Lagoon area as well as along many roadsides in North County.

(left)
Dew Drops

Marie Tartar

NIKON N90S
VELVIA
F5.6

Dewdrops from a brilliantly colored Zauschneria, are frozen in time at Cardiff-by-the-Sea.

(opposite)
Smokey Reflection

Marie Tartar

NIKON N90S
SENSIA
F5.6

A wildflower floats in San Elijo Lagoon and is set off by unusual cloud and sky reflections.

Lacey Grasses

Marie Tartar

NIKON N90S
KODACHROME
F4

Pennisetum fountain grasses, growing on a Cardiff
bluff overlooking San Elijo Lagoon, glow pink in the
light of the setting sun.

(opposite)

On Stage

Marie Tartar

NIKON N90S
KODACHROME
F5.6

Changing colors catch the viewer's eye in a dramatic
show of clouds, sky and sunset reflected in the waters
at San Elijo Lagoon.

Beauty and the Beast

Isabella Breasted

A wave breaks over the wall at the parking lot on Restaurant Row in Cardiff-by-the-Sea.

(left)
Misty Morning

Mary L. Thompson
CANON REBEL G

A misty morning at Solana Beach finds a visitor gazing at the foggy seascape with lifeguard stations in the background.

(opposite)
Colorful Walkway

James Blank
PENTAX 67
EKTACHROME64
F 16 1/60

Colorful flowers line the walkway of this beautiful park.

Reminiscent of Days of Old

Carol Cirone

CANON ELAN PROVIA 100
28-80MM LENS

Designed by San Diego architect Rob Guigley,
this train station was inspired by old military
housing used in Solana Beach during WWII.

Gulls Reflection

Geoff Shester

NIKON N90S
SENSIA
F32

The sunset lights up the cliffs of Solana Beach as two
seagulls, reflected in the wet sand, watch the day
come to an end.

right)

Del Mar Racetrack

Geoff Shester

CANON A1
FUJI PROVIA 100F
F4

The Del Mar Fairgrounds has been a hot spot for horse
racing since the early days when Jimmy Durante and
Bing Crosby first opened the track in 1937. This photo
was taken from the old Highway 1 looking across the
railroad tracks.

Polo Anyone?

Isabella Breasted

NIKON N-70 35MM
KODAK 200

The imposing gate of the San Diego Polo Club frames one of the many multi-colored hot air balloons that take off from the grounds in the early morning hours.

Del Mar Race Track

Isabella Breasted

NIKON N6006
300MM LENS
KODAK 200

Del Mar Race Track and Fairgrounds is nestled in the valley by the railroad tracks and old Highway 101.

Solana Beach

James Blank

PENTAX 67
EKTACHROME 64
F 16 AT 60

A view of the Solana Beach coastline is framed by tree limbs.

Popular Sport

Isabella Breasted

NIKON 6006
300MM LENS
KODAK 200
AUTO FOCUS

Surfing is one of the most popular year-round sports along Cardiff-by-the-Sea.

Lone Seagull

Isabella Breasted

NIKON 6006
300MM LENS
KODAK 200
AUTO FOCUS

A lone seagull flies above the setting sun at Cardiff-by-the-Sea.

(opposite)
Storm Break

Isabella Breasted

NIKON 6006
300MM LENS
KODAK 200
AUTO FOCUS

A streak of sunlight breaks through the clouds to bathe the bluffs along old Highway 101 in Cardiff-by-the-Sea.

encinitas
leucadia

Living on High

Mary L. Thompson

CANON REBEL G
AUTO

These two boats which appear to be in dry dock, are really private homes designed by Mile M. Kellogg and are nestled on a street in Encinitas.

(left)

Mysterious Night

Marie Tartar

NIKON N-70
KODAK 200
AUTO

Golden rays from a sunset reflect on the sand and waters off the cliffs of Swami's Beach. A mysterious light glows through the dark rugged cliffs.

(opposite)

Stately Palms

Marie Tartar

NIKON N90S
SENSIA
F16

Palm trees accentuate the view of Swami's Beach along the Encinitas coast.

Double Cross

Richard E. Leffler

CANON A1/100-300MM
SENSIA 100

Each day in the town of Encinitas, this photographic image of Saints Constantine and Helen Greek Orthodox Church and the "double cross" are played out with the help of the sun against the golden dome.

(right)

Symbols of Encinitas

Marie Tartar

NIKON N90S
SENSIA
F11

Three of the familiar symbols of Encinitas are depicted together in this photograph of palm trees, the mosque towers of the Self-Realization Fellowship (locally known as Swami's), and a surfer's crossing sign.

(opposite, top)

Moonlight Beach

Joseph M. Libertini

DIGITAL OLYMPUS D600L

The sunset backlights the silhouette of a palm in this photo at Moonlight Beach in Encinitas.

(opposite, bottom)

Woody Reflection

Carol Cirone

CANON 1-N 20-35MM
PROVIA 100

Owners of "Woody" automobiles convene annually at Moonlight State Beach. A mirror image of one woody is reflected in the polished body of its mate.

Reflection Pond

Melvyn W. Forman

LEICA R8
KODACHROME 64
F22

A reflection pond nestled in the solitude of the meditation gardens at the Self Realization Fellowship. The gardens are open to the public and visitors are asked to respect the serene setting.

(left)

Koi Pond

Mary L. Thompson

CANON REBEL G
AUTO

This koi pond is surrounded by lovely gardens.

(opposite)

Quail Botanical Gardens

Mary L. Thompson

CANON REBEL G
AUTO

A tropical paradise covering 30 acres of hills and valleys in Encinitas, Quail Botanical Gardens is a Garden of Eden for plant enthusiasts, photographers and other visitors. The park contains over 3000 varieties of unusual botanical specimens. Don't forget your camera!

Birth of a Butterfly

Paul Shilling

CANON ELAN IIE
KODAK E100VS

A monarch butterfly minutes after emerging from its chrysalis.

(below)

Swallow Tail Butterfly

Paul Shilling

CANON ELAN IIE
KODAK E200

A swallowtail butterfly lies suspended against the contrasting reds and greens of the Egyptian Star Cluster plant.

Young Monarch

Paul Shilling

CANON ELAN IIE
KODAK E200

A monarch butterfly is resting atop an Egyptian
Star-Cluster at The Monarch Program in Encinitas.

Foggy Night

Isabella Breasted

NIKON 6006 300MM
KODAK 200
AUTO

A glimpse of the setting sun provides a quiet escape as viewed through the muted hues of a foggy night.

(below)
Beach Fun

James Blank

PENTAX 67
EKTACHROME 64
F11 1/125

Crowds of sun worshipers gather on Moonlight Beach in Encinitas.

(opposite)
Fish Head

Isabella Breasted

NIKON 6006 300MM
KODAK 200
AUTO

The outline of the ocean ledge creates an image of a fish head with the surfer as the eye of the fish.

Heading Home

Shirley A. Reynolds

MINOLTA WEATHERMATIC DUAL 35
KODAK EBX

A solitary surfer heads home after a satisfying day
riding the waves.

(top)

Tide pools

Shirley A. Reynolds

OLYMPUS OM1
KODAK ELITE CHROME II

Kids and adults alike enjoy exploring sea life found in the exposed tide pools at Swami's Beach in Encinitas

(bottom)

Blazing Sunset

Isabella Breasted

NIKON 6006 300MM
KODAK 200
AUTO

This blazing sunset seems to meld the sky with the sea.

Labyrinth Walkers

Kirk Van Allen

CANON

Leucadian Labyrinth Walkers are retracing the pattern drawn on a canvas of sand by the artist Kirkos at Beacon's Beach.

(left)
Threatening Clouds Offshore

Gunnar Ostrand

NIKON N70/28-200MM LENS
FUJI SENSIA
F11

Threatening clouds hover over a steel-gray sea.

Surfers Trail

James Blank

PENTAX 67
EKTACHROME 64
F 16 1/60

Surfers head down the trail along a flower-covered
cliff at a beach in Leucadia.

Olivenhain Meeting House

Thomas J. Kovtan

NIKON N90S
FUJI REALA
F8

The landmark Olivenhain Meeting House is located at the intersection of Rancho Santa Fe and 7th Street in Encinitas. The town council continues to meet here every Wednesday.

Kelp Poppers

Rosalee Anderson

NIKON FE
ASA 200
F16

Swami's seaweed, a cool ocean breeze, and sand between your toes create a relaxing place at Swami's Beach. The urge to stop and pop a few of those pods is simply irresistible.

Catch Me If You Can

Rosalee Anderson

NIKON FE
ASA 200
F11

Sandpipers scurry before the incoming waves.

carlsbad
oceanside

Carlsbad Shops

Mary L. Thompson
CANON REBEL G
AUTO

A quaint community peppered with small shops and restaurants, Carlsbad was originally named Frazier's Station after Captain John A. Frazier.

(left)

**Newman's Restaurant
(Old Twin Inns)**

Josh Ritter
SUPER SPEED CERAPHIC
AGFA CHROME 50
1 MIN @F16

Neiman's Restaurant (Formerly The Twin Inns) was built as a Victorian residence in 1887. The twin residences were remodeled in 1914 as a hotel.

Historical Carlsbad Train Station

Geoff Shester

CANON A1
FUJI VELVIA
F5.6

The original train station, built in 1887, has
served many functions such as a stagecoach
depot, a post office, a general store, and a
telegraph station. It now serves as the
Carlsbad Visitor's Bureau.

Bursts of Color

Mary L. Thompson

CANON REBEL G
AUTO

Eight million tiny bursts of color explode
in symmetrical rows to delight the eyes of
residents and visitors.

(left)
Ribbons of Color

Josh Ritter

SUPER SPEED CERAPHIC
FUJICHROME 50
1/30@F22

Over fifty acres of ranunculus blossoms form
ribbons of color along the hillside of the
Carlsbad Flower Fields. Anderson's Windmill
(formerly part of Anderson's Pea Soup
Restaurant) is nestled among the trees and
buildings in the background providing a touch
of Denmark to the area.

Center stage

James Blank

PENTAX 67
EKTACHROME 64
F22 1/30

Two young girls take center stage in the splendor of color surrounding them. Photographers flock to the fields in the springtime to take advantage of the colorful setting.

Silver Lining

Mary L. Thompson

CANON REBEL G
AUTO

Shimmering silver tones of the
ocean and clouds appear as a new
day breaks.

A World of Color

Goran Matijasevic
WIDELUX
KODAK EKTACHROME 100

The Grand Pacific Palisades Hotel overlooks a
corner of the flower fields.

Palette of Color

Rosalee Anderson

NIKON FM
ASA200
F11

The Carlsbad Flower Fields draw huge crowds to enjoy the rainbows of ranunculus in full bloom.

(below)
Cascade of Color

Rosalee Anderson

NIKON FM
ASA200
F8

Colorful ranunculus cascade down the hillside of the flower fields annually. Colors are kept separate because 98% of the flowers are grown for the sale of their bulbs.

Sea of Color

James Blank

PENTAX 67
EKTACHROME 64
F16 1/60

The ranunculus flowers spread across the hillside. Plantings are timed to afford a continuous bloom cycle during the springtime. In 1933, Edwin Frazee began an enterprise in San Diego County that has since expanded to the hills of Carlsbad.

(below)

Anxious to Move On

Diana Curry

CANNON Z115
KODAK 200

Visitors of all ages enjoy the beauty of the flower fields.

Delectable Fare

Geoff Shester

CANON A1
FUJI VELVIA
F5.6

A Great Egret searches for delicacies at the Carlsbad
tide pools. Several species of shorebirds are common
in this area.

Carlsbad Beach

Goran Matijasevic

WIDELUX
FUJICHROME SENSIA

Wispy clouds add a touch of motion to this typical
scene of visitors walking along a sandy stretch
of beach.

Colorful Composition

Sharon McCallum

NIKON N70 35-135MM
FUJICHROME VELVIA
F8

The intricacies of engineering are exemplified in the
silhouette of the pier as it rests against the backdrop
of a parfait sky.

Picture Perfect

Shirley A. Reynolds

CANON EOS S2E

The end of a perfect day is captured on film at
Oceanside Harbor.

Resting

Shirley A. Reynolds
CANON EOS S2E/70-300MM

Pelicans and seagulls line the docks at Oceanside Harbor.

(below)
Winter Surf

Shirley A. Reynolds
CANON EOS A2E
KODAK EBX

In winter, surfers brave the cold air and water with wetsuits to surf beside the Oceanside Pier.

Oceanside Harbor
Honorable Mention

James Blank
PENTAX 67
EKTACHROME 64
F8.5 1/125

The gentle movement of a kayaker breaks
the still waters of Oceanside Harbor.

COASTER

Four Flags

Richard E. Leffler

CANON T70/24MMPOLARIZER
IMATION 100
F11

The photographer captured a rare sight on this day
as he noticed four flags flying in front of the mission,
representing the United States, California, Spain
and Mexico.

(right)

On His Way

Richard E. Leffler

CANON A1/300
SENSIA

Mission San Luis Rey de Francia, called "King of the
Missions" because of its size and namesake, was
founded in 1798. The timelessness of the mission is
reflected in the simplicity of this scene.

(opposite)

Coaster

Thomas J. Kovtan

NIKON N90S
KODAK 160VC
F5.6

The Coaster began commuter service in 1995 and
runs Monday through Saturday between Oceanside
and San Diego. It's a great way to see San Diego's
North County Coast.

Holiday Reflection

Shirley A. Reynolds

CANON EOS A2E
KODAK

Every December, North County mariners light up their
boats and cruise around Oceanside Harbor in the
Holiday Boat Parade of Lights.

Starbursts of Light

Josh Ritter

SUPER SPEED CERAPHIC
EKTACHROME 100
8 MIN.@F32

Starbursts of light cast a glow to the 1,942-foot
Oceanside Municipal Pier. Because of its length, golf
carts are often used for transportation along the pier.

Silhouettes at Sunset

Sharon McCallum

NIKON N70 35-135MM
FUJICHROME VELVIA
F8

The Oceanside Municipal Pier was first build around 1890
and restored in 1987. The pastel glow erases the line of
the horizon to make water and sky appear as one.

contributors

Steve Abuzzo
4174 Blackton Drive
La Mesa, CA 91941
18, 19

Roger Alther
848 N. Mollison D-7
El Cajon, CA 92021
66

Rosalee Anderson
4416 Cinto Cristalino
San Diego, CA 92117
107 (2), 116 (2)

Garry Belinsky
5985 Dandridge Lane #83
San Diego, CA 92115
44, 58

Zackery Birdsell
2028 3rd Ave. Apt. B
San Diego, CA 92101
45

James Blank
1110 Red Maple Drive
Chula Vista, CA 91910
*cover, back cover, 1, 22, 23, 27,
28, 29, 50, 51, 52, 53, 55, 63, 83,
87, 100, 105, 113, 117, 123*

Michael Boidy
6189 Montezuma
San Diego, CA 92115
64

Isabella Breasted
112 Roper Court
Encinitas, CA 92024-2905
*37, 39, 62 (2), 82, 86 (2),
88 (2), 89, 100, 101, 103*

Caroline E. Brown
1009 Greystone Circle
Morgantown, WV 26508
34, 38 (2), 65, 66, 67

Carol Cirone
8788 Britt Court
San Diego, CA 92123
34, 35, 36 (2), 61, 70, 84, 94

Jim Cline
11223-5 Carmel Creek Road
San Diego, CA 92130
10–11, 56, 57

Diana Curry
1824 Caymen Way
Vista, CA
117

Melvyn W. Forman
17310 Cleeco Place
Poway, CA 92064
96

Richard Grafton
3695 Fenelon Street
San Diego, CA 92106
47

Diane Hotz
1234 Loring Street
San Diego, CA. 92109
26

Ryan Kelly
11692 Carmel Creek Road #N202
San Diego, CA 92130
14, 17, 30

Thomas J. Kovtan
9669 Gold Coast Drive
San Diego, CA 92126
32, 72 (2), 106, 124

Tiger Lee
4118 Raya Way
San Diego, CA 92122
31

Richard E. Leffler
8401 Tio Diego Place
La Mesa, CA 91941
59, 75 (2), 95, 125 (2)

Joseph M. Libertini
2637 Galicia Way
Carlsbad, CA 92009
94

Lindsey P. Martin
135 N. Main Street
Hurricane, UT 84737
9, 56, 60, 71, 76

Goran Matijasevic
420 S. La Esperanza
San Clemente, CA 92672
46, 115, 119

Joanne Max
13164 Winstanley Way
San Diego, CA 92130
77 (2)

Sharon McCallum
10509 Challenge Boulevard
La Mesa, CA 91941
120, 127

Gunnar Ostrand
5673-A Lake Murray Boulevard
La Mesa, CA. 91942
33, 73, 104

Lindsey Padgett
3035 Thorn Street
San Diego, CA 92104
7

Bill Remlinger
1931 Julianna Street
El Cajon, CA 92019
15, 20–21, 24 (2), 25, 54

Shirley A. Reynolds
4093 Galbar Street
Oceanside, CA 92056
*26, 70, 102, 103, 121,
122 (2), 126*

Josh Ritter
3077 State Street
Carlsbad, CA 92008
110, 112, 126

Geoff Shester
400 Western Drive
Santa Cruz, CA 95060
*42, 48–49, 60, 74, 85 (2),
111, 118*

Paul Shilling
3969 Caminito Del Mar Surf
San Diego, CA 92130
65, 98 (2), 99

Marie Tartar
2598 Montgomery Avenue
Cardiff, CA 92007
*16 (2), 78 (2), 79, 80, 81, 92,
93, 95*

Mary L. Thompson
3700 10th Avenue Apt. 3C
San Diego, CA 92103
*30, 82, 92, 96, 97, 110,
112, 114*

Kirk Van Allen
461 Naiad Street
Encinitas, CA 92024
104

Rick Wiley
Beaver Lake Drive
San Diego, 92119
43